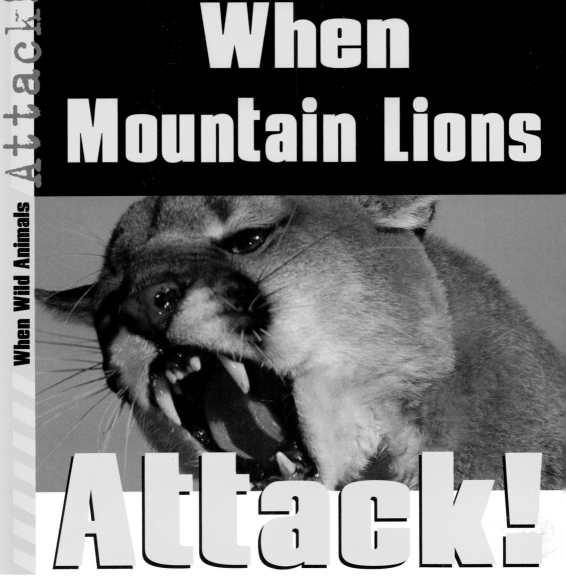

When
Mountain Lions
Attack!

When Wild Animals **Attack!**

Sarah Hansen

Enslow Publishers, Inc.
40 Industrial Road
Box 398
Berkeley Heights, NJ 07922
USA

http://www.enslow.com

Library of Congress Cataloging-in-Publication Data

Hansen, Sarah.
  When mountain lions attack! / by Sarah Hansen.
     p. cm. — (When wild animals attack!)
  Includes bibliographical references and index.
  ISBN 0-7660-2668-X
  1. Puma attacks—Juvenile literature. I. Title. II. Series.
  QL737.C23H3555 2006
  599.75'241566—dc22
                                        2006011694

Printed in the United States of America

10 9 8 7 6 5 4 3 2 1

To Our Readers:
We have done our best to make sure all Internet Addresses in this book were active and appropriate when we went to press. However, the author and the publisher have no control over and assume no liability for the material available on those Internet sites or on other Web sites they may link to. Any comments or suggestions can be sent by e-mail to comments@enslow.com or to the address on the back cover.

Photo Credits: Associated Press, The Salinas Californian, p. 25; Associated Press, UC Davis, pp. 3, 39; CORBIS/W. Perry Conway, p. 15; CORBIS/Terry W. Eggers, pp. 10, 14; CORBIS/ D. Robert & Lorri Franz, p. 33; CORBIS/Orange County Register/Mark Avery, p. 37; Corel Stock Photos, pp. 3, 23, 44; Getty Images/Aurora, p. 31; Getty Images/National Geographic, pp. 3, 4, 12, 17, 20, 26, 34; Getty Images/Stone, p. 40; iStockphoto.com/James Phelps, p. 43; Photo Researchers Inc./ Gregory G. Dimijian, M.D., pp. 3, 29; Photo Researchers Inc./ George D. Lepp, p. 1; Photo Researchers Inc./Kent Wood, p. 6; Photos.com, pp. 3, 11, 32, 42, 45.

Illustration: Kevin Davidson, p.19

Cover Photos: Photo Researchers Inc./George D. Lepp (front), Photos.com (back)

Contents

One

Mountain lions are excellent at both hunting and climbing. They use their thick tails for balance.

The Hunter Becomes the Hunted

Clarence Hall's job was to hunt for animals that killed livestock such as cattle. This made him an expert at tracking and hunting mountain lions. Like all skilled hunters, Hall learned about his prey. He came to admire the mountain lion, calling it "the shyest creature on the North American Continent."

But on a cold Canadian winter day in January 2000, the tables turned. Clarence Hall, then in his mid-seventies, became the hunted one.

Hall received a report that a dog had been killed by a mountain lion near Bella Coola, British Columbia. Hall went out early to look for the tracks of the mountain lion. He did not think it would still be in the area.

So he was shocked to see an adult mountain lion just forty feet from him. It was curled up by a tree, swishing its tail back and forth. Knowing that sudden movement might cause the mountain lion to attack, Hall slowly crept back toward his car, more than 150 feet away. He was

Many Names for the Mountain Lion

The mountain lion has been given many different names by the various people living in its vast range. Native Americans often had names for the mountain lion that showed their respect for it. For example, the Chickasaw, who lived in what is now Mississippi and Tennessee, called it Koe-Ishto, or "cat of god." The Cherokee name for it, Klandaghi, means "lord of the forest." In the Southwest, the Hopi referred to the mountain lion as the "guardian of the tribe."

Some of the names used in the United States today for the mountain lion came from South America. The Guarani of Brazil called it *cuguacuarana*, which became "cougar" in English. Puma, another named used today, came from the Inca, and means "a powerful animal."

Mountain lion, cougar, and puma are the most common names in the western United States today. In the East, the names panther, painter, and catamount are also used. The mountain lion's scientific name is *Puma concolor*, which means "cat of one color."

An ancient Anasazi drawing of a mountain lion in New Mexico.

almost there when he was suddenly struck from behind. Later, Hall said it felt like a baseball bat had slammed the back of his neck.

Stunned, Hall lay in the snow. Blood ran into his ears and down his shoulders. The mountain lion's long canine teeth dug deeply into his neck. For an instant the mountain lion let go, but then grabbed Hall's neck again and began shaking him

The mountain lion grabbed the man's neck and began shaking him in its jaws.

in its jaws. From the first moment Hall had spotted it, the mountain lion had not made a sound.

Hall remembered hearing that if a dog ever attacks, you should try to grip it behind the canine teeth on the lower jaw. Without waiting another second, Hall reached back and put his right thumb in one side of the mountain lion's mouth and the fingers of his left hand in the other side. He pulled down, and it worked! The mountain lion's teeth were out of his neck, but now they were cutting up his hands.

Hall wrestled the mountain lion's head around to the front of him and tried to choke the animal with his left arm. His plan was to push its head into the snow so it could not breathe. Before he could do that, a man came running with a rifle. The man fired four shots. Finally, Hall felt the mountain lion go limp.

Hall later said, "The mountain lion had every reason to attack me. He was starving. There was nothing in his stomach but water, and porcupine quills in his throat. . . . He was in pain. And when I put my hands on either side of his face, and I looked straight into his eyes, I felt sorry: That was the closest I've ever gotten to such a fierce animal, and I saw how beautiful an animal this was, and I felt sorry that it had to be destroyed."

Increasing Attacks

Such frightening attacks make it easy to look at the mountain lion as a vicious enemy of humans. But that is not true. As Clarence Hall noted, the mountain lion that attacked him was probably a hungry animal in search of something to eat.

Mountain lions can survive in many kinds of places, from high, rugged mountains to swampy jungles. In past centuries, they could be found all the way from Canada to the southern tip of South America, and from the Pacific coast to the Atlantic coast. In fact, at one time their range was larger than that of any other mammal in the Western Hemisphere.

In the early American colonies of the 17th and 18th centuries, settlers rarely saw mountain

What Sounds Do Mountain Lions Make?

People have sometimes mistaken the sounds of mountain lion kittens for birds. The kittens make cheeping sounds, screeches, or soft whistles. Adult mountain lions also make whistling and cheeping sounds. They seem to communicate with their kittens this way.

Mountain lions also purr, similar to the purring of a domestic cat, when they are relaxed and contented. When threatened, adult mountain lions hiss, growl, and snarl. The legendary mountain lion scream is said to sound like a piercing shriek. In fact, this scream is very rarely heard in the wild, and some scientists suggest that mountain lions probably make this sound only during mating.

lions. But they heard their screams in the night and were afraid that they would harm their livestock. The folklore around mountain lions became overblown. There were tales of mountain lions clawing at log cabins or trying to get down chimneys to steal children. In Maine, mountain lions were said to crack their victims' skulls with a bony ball at the end of their tails. Another story from New England described a mountain lion with tusks that were four feet long. Mountain lions were

Mountain lion habitats, like this one in Montana, include rugged wilderness. Here, a mother teaches her kitten to hunt.

hunted and killed by the thousands throughout the 1800s and 1900s. But in spite of their fierce reputation, mountain lions usually avoided people, mostly staying out of sight.

It is still very rare to see a mountain lion, but the number of encounters between mountain lions and humans is increasing. Experts say there have been two to three times more mountain lion encounters since the early 1990s than in previous decades. People are continually moving further into mountain lion territory.

A Shrinking Range

The range of the mountain lion, or the area in which the species lives, is much smaller now than it was a few hundred years ago, when it roamed over most of the Western Hemisphere. Today in the United States, stable populations of mountain lions are found only in Texas, Florida, and the twelve states west of the Rocky Mountains. Mountain lions also live in the western Canadian province of British Columbia.

In Florida, where these animals are called panthers, there are fewer than fifty left.

TWO

Even a large rabbit like this one is small prey
for a mountain lion. A mountain lion's main prey is deer.

An Expert Hunter

Mountain lions are highly successful hunters. All of a mountain lion's features, from its powerful jaws to the color of its coat, help it to hunt and kill its prey, or food.

Mountain lions are carnivores, or meat-eaters. They eat deer more than any other meat. They also sometimes eat elk, bighorn sheep, wild pigs, bobcats, coyotes, mountain goats, antelope, and even bear.

It is most efficient for mountain lions to kill one of these big animals and get a lot of meat from a single kill. But they also kill and eat smaller animals, such as armadillos, beavers, porcupines, squirrels, rabbits, skunks, raccoons, birds, and foxes.

A mountain lion's tan or sandy brown fur provides good camouflage. It easily blends in with the undergrowth or rocks where the mountain lion hides to stalk its prey. Mountain lions vary in size from about 80 to 130 pounds for females, to 110 to 180 pounds for males. Some mountain lions can weigh over 200 pounds, but these are unusual. An average female is about six feet long, including the tail, while an average male is seven feet long.

A mountain lion's powerful muscles give it the speed and strength it needs to bring down large animals such as deer and elk. Its jaws are very strong, allowing it to kill its prey with the sharp canine teeth on the sides of its mouth.

A mountain lion's eyes see best at night and at dawn and dusk, the times when it normally hunts for food. A mountain lion also uses its ears, which it can move together, as well as separately, to detect sounds coming from different directions when it is searching for prey.

A mountain lion uses its long, sharp canine teeth to kill prey.

A mountain lion in Colorado chases a mule deer, trying to attack it from the side.

Mountain lions hunt by ambush, meaning that they sneak up on their prey to take it by surprise. For example, a mountain lion may lie on rocks near a trail where prey is likely to pass. When the mountain lion sees its prey, it begins to stalk it, crouching low to the ground. It may stop and stay completely still for as long as half an hour, always watching its target.

When the mountain lion is within fifty feet of its prey, it is time to attack. It springs forward, taking long leaps or running very fast. A mountain lion most often attacks from the rear or the side, grabbing the neck and shoulders of the prey with its front claws. A quick bite to the neck might kill the prey instantly, or sever a large vein in the neck which causes the prey to bleed to death.

Saving Some for Later

After it has killed an animal, a mountain lion will usually drag the carcass to a safe place to feed. When it has had enough, it stands over the carcass and uses its front claws to rake pine needles and sticks over it to cover it up. This is known as creating a "cache," and protects the food from other animals such as coyotes and vultures. The mountain lion may stay in the area for a few days, returning to the carcass to eat and to keep other animals away. Sometimes a mountain lion will move the cache before each feeding, dragging it hundreds of feet to a new place before it eats. This ensures that the cache stays hidden from other animals who might have discovered it.

A Mountain Lion's Life

A female mountain lion finds a den in which to give birth, such as under a fallen log or in a small cave. She usually gives birth to two or three kittens.

Mountain lion kittens weigh less than a pound when they are born. They begin nursing on their mother's milk when they are only a few minutes old, and double their weight within three weeks. Their fur is covered with black spots the size of pennies. These markings will provide good camouflage for the first few months of their lives, before they gradually fade away. This camouflage is important to protect the kittens from predators when their mother is away from the den searching for food.

At first, the growing kittens stay close to the den. Already they are beginning to stalk anything that moves, such as grasshoppers and weeds swaying in the wind. They stalk and pounce on one another, fighting with teeth and claws. They are playing, and at the same time they are developing skills that will later be useful in hunting their own food.

The mother mountain lion brings chunks of meat to the kittens while they are still nursing.

A mother mountain lion brings a rabbit to her spotted kittens. She will teach them how to feed on the prey.

Mountain Lion
FACTs

Experts agree that mountain lions vary greatly in size. Here are some general figures:

Height: Males average 30 inches (two and a half feet) tall at the shoulder. Females are about 27 inches tall at the shoulder.

Weight: Males are 110 to 180 pounds, while females are 80 to 130 pounds.

Length: Males may be more than seven feet long, including the tail. Females are generally up to six feet long.

Color: Tan or sandy brown. Kittens are covered with black spots.

Range: Texas, Florida, states west of the Rocky Mountains, southwestern Canada.

Then, when they are about two months old, they will begin to follow her to the site of a kill. There, they see how their mother gets the flesh from the carcass. They see that when they are finished feeding, she covers the rest of the carcass with sticks and brush.

For the next few months the kittens continue to practice their hunting skills. As they get older and stronger, they will even go off hunting on their own for a few days at a time. Finally, when they are

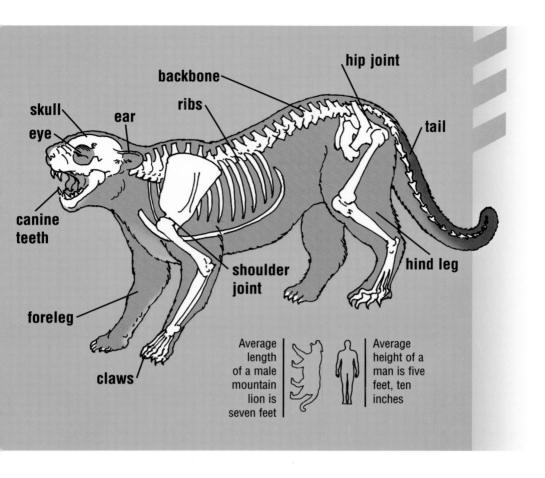

skull
eye
ear
backbone
ribs
hip joint
tail
canine teeth
shoulder joint
hind leg
foreleg
claws

Average length of a male mountain lion is seven feet

Average height of a man is five feet, ten inches

between twelve and eighteen months old, it is time for them to leave the litter for the last time.

They will live the solitary life of adult mountain lions until it is time to mate. When they are two to three years old, a male usually seeks out a female. The pair may stay together for as long as two weeks before going their separate ways again after mating. About three months later, the female will give birth to her kittens and the cycle starts all over again.

Three

A mountain lion focuses on its prey as it runs toward it.

A Young Lion Attacks

In the spring of 1998, Andy Peterson was hiking in Colorado's Roxborough State Park. He was an experienced hiker and a state park ranger, so he was not afraid to be hiking alone.

Peterson was heading down a trail when he came upon a small mountain lion chewing on a stick. At first Peterson felt lucky to see such a rare sight. Then, realizing the danger, he was afraid. Peterson slowly and quietly backed up the trail. He carefully reached for his pocketknife. He looked down at it and thought the small blade would not do him much good if he was attacked.

Once the mountain lion saw Peterson, it watched him intently. It started moving toward him. Typical of an attacking lion, it kept its eyes locked on the man.

Peterson knew to make himself look as big as possible so that the mountain lion would not think he was easy prey. He jumped up and down, waving his arms and shouting at the mountain lion. But the mountain lion kept moving forward. When

Peterson shouted and backed further away, the mountain lion followed.

Then Peterson watched in horror as the lion squinted, bared its teeth, and flattened its ears. Suddenly it growled and jumped with its front legs extended forward, knocking Peterson over. They rolled together down the trail. Peterson jumped up and the cat leaped again, this time missing him altogether.

Now Peterson was bleeding, stumbling down the trail. He tried to hit the mountain lion with his pack, but missed every time as the lion easily ducked out of the way.

Suddenly the path dropped off steeply into boulders, and Peterson jumped, and then fell, down through the rocks. The mountain lion leaped into the air again and landed on Peterson just as he hit the ground below the boulders. They rolled down the path again.

This time when they stopped Peterson could not jump free. He found himself kneeling over the mountain lion, which was on its back. His head was partially inside the mountain lion's mouth, its teeth sunk into his skull. He could see a large tooth an inch from his left eye.

Blood poured down Peterson's face. He still had the knife in his hand, so he tried to cut the mountain lion's throat. But the animal clawed at his face and did not seem to notice the knife.

A Mountain Lion's Moves

Mountain lions are built to move easily over rough, uneven ground and to jump long distances in one bound. Their light, flexible backbones and muscular legs allow for both quick turns and long strides, while their heavy tails help them keep their balance. They are also athletic jumpers. Mountain lions have been known to leap more than forty feet to catch prey on the ground, and at least fifteen feet straight up to a tree limb or a high rock ledge.

A mountain lion's back legs are longer than its front legs, and experts believe that this may be part of the reason that these cats can jump so well. When it comes to climbing trees, some

scientists say that mountain lions are the best climbers of all the wild cats. They can easily scale tree trunks, as well as climb through branches to the tops of trees two hundred to three hundred feet off the ground.

At that moment Peterson realized that his right hand was touching the mountain lion's eye. He poked his thumb as hard as he could into the lion's eye, and at the same time stabbed its skull with the knife.

The mountain lion shrieked and jumped backward, letting go of Peterson. Peterson quickly threw a large rock at the lion. He backed down the trail until he was out of sight. Then he turned and ran. A few minutes later he met some hikers on the trail.

Peterson was taken to a hospital by helicopter. Doctors used seventy staples to close his head wounds, and several dozen stitches in his face, neck, chest, shoulders, and right leg.

Less than a year later, a mountain lion missing its right eye was seen about fifteen miles from where Peterson had been attacked. The police tranquilized it (put it to sleep temporarily) and moved it to a location farther away from people.

A Dangerous Young Lion

Many attacks on humans involve two- to three-year-old mountain lions. The small mountain lion that attacked Andy Peterson was probably one of these. A young mountain lion out on its own for the first time is more likely than other mountain lions to run into trouble with humans.

Though still very unusual, there are two reasons why people are more likely to encounter a

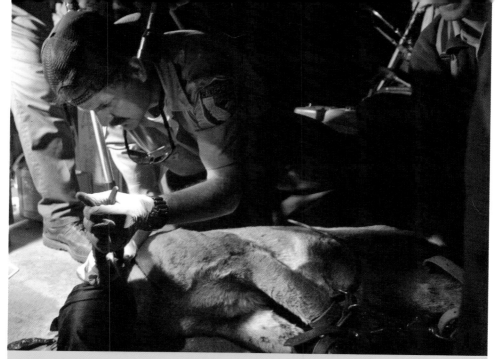

A wildlife biologist tags the ear of a tranquilized mountain lion in California after it wandered into a residential area. The tag will allow biologists to identify the mountain lion in the future.

young mountain lion than an older one. First, a younger lion does not have a lot of experience hunting food on its own. Until it gains more experience and has more success as a hunter, a young mountain lion may often be hungry and more likely to view humans as prey.

Secondly, it has recently left its mother's home range and will have to travel for many weeks or months before it finds a place where it will not be competing with other mountain lions for food. Always on the move, a young mountain lion is more likely to pass through areas where there are people.

Four

In the mountains of Idaho, a mountain lion takes
a break after hunting and killing a duck.

A Hungry Mountain Lion

On May 25, 1998, Mary Jane Coder and her three young daughters were hiking in Big Bend National Park in South Texas. Coder was just about to take a picture when she heard one of her children screaming. She turned around to see what was wrong. Not five feet away from her children was a mountain lion. It was crouched low. It looked like it was ready to attack.

Coder quickly pulled her daughters behind her and threw a rock at the big cat. It just hissed at them. She told her daughters to get her pocketknife out of a nearby backpack. Then she started yelling at the mountain lion, waving the knife at it. That did not seem to alarm the mountain lion. Instead, it lunged at the girls.

The frightened girls ran in different directions, and the mountain lion went after them one at a time. Each time it charged at one of them, their mother would run toward the mountain lion and chase it away, screaming at it and shouting at the girls to gather behind her.

Once, the mountain lion got so close it clawed Coder's hand.

Finally, not knowing what else to do, mother and children huddled under a rock ledge. The mountain lion jumped onto a rock right above them and stayed there, waiting. Coder, terrified for her life and the lives of her children, tried to figure out what to do next.

The mountain lion jumped onto a rock right above them and stayed there, waiting.

Their car was two miles away and they were trapped by the mountain lion. The big cat might get tired of waiting and attack them in their hiding place. If she fought the mountain lion and got hurt, Coder thought, her children would be helpless and would probably be killed. With no good choices before her, she decided that they should try to get to the car.

Coder thought that maybe the mountain lion would not try to attack them if they stayed close together. Cautiously they left their hiding place and walked together in a tight group. Coder walked backward with her knife open, keeping her eye on the mountain lion. As she predicted, it did not try to attack them.

When they could no longer see the mountain lion, they started to think they were out of danger.

Big Bend National Park in Texas is prime mountain lion territory. Smart hikers know that one way to keep mountain lions away is to make noise while hiking.

But then the youngest child screamed. There was the mountain lion, crouched in the underbrush ahead! It had circled around and was waiting for them.

But again the mountain lion did not attack. It stayed crouched by the trail as they passed. There is no way to know for sure why the mountain lion did not try to attack the group again. Their tight huddle may have seemed too difficult to try to

Shared Habitat: Predator and Prey

A mountain lion's habitat needs to have cover, or places to hide when stalking and attacking prey. Good cover for a mountain lion includes rock outcroppings and boulders as well as brush consisting of small trees, bushes, and thick weeds.

A mountain lion's habitat must also be a good place for deer or other prey animals to live. Deer need dense areas of undergrowth in which to hide from predators and raise their young. They also need trees to shelter them from wind and cold, and to provide shade on the hottest days. In addition, deer need many different kinds of plants to eat.

Mountain lions benefit from sharing a habitat with deer. Scientists think that the deer benefit as well because mountain lions keep the deer population under control. For example, if all the deer lived to produce young, there would not be enough food to go around. Some would starve. Predators such as mountain lions help to keep nature in balance.

divide. The family eventually made their way to the car without any harm.

Coder was treated for the wound on her hand. The trail and nearby campsites were closed. But the park rangers did not hunt down and kill the mountain lion. Coder was glad about that. She said that the animal was just "doing what mountain lions do."

Attacking out of Hunger

At the time of the attack on Coder and her daughters, there had been a severe drought (a long, dry period without rain) in the area. Park rangers said that the mountain lion might have gone after the family because it could not find its normal food. In this part of Texas a mountain lion's main prey are deer and wild pigs. Because there had not been enough rain, there were not as many plants for the deer and wild pigs to eat. Many of these prey

Wild pigs are a mountain lion's main prey in the area around Big Bend National Park.

animals had possibly moved to other areas seeking food. That meant less food for a mountain lion.

Like all wild animals, mountain lions have to work for their food. When they stalk and kill other animals, they are doing what they must do to survive. A healthy mountain lion needs to eat an average of one deer or other large animal per week. A female mountain lion caring for kittens needs almost twice as much meat. When it cannot find the food it usually eats, a mountain lion has to look for other food. Fortunately, Mary Jane Coder and her three daughters did not become a meal for the mountain lion they encountered.

A mother mountain lion caring for her kittens must hunt for much more meat than other mountain lions. This mother is carrying one of her kittens.

How a Mountain Lion Eats

After a mountain lion brings down a deer or other prey it usually drags the carcass to a sheltered place to feed. First it rips a hole in the hide with its teeth and claws to get to the meat. Then it tears out the prey's intestines and organs and eats the heart, lungs, and liver. These organs have more vitamins, fat, and protein than the rest of the animal. All of these things are good for a mountain lion's diet.

If the mountain lion is not interrupted, it eats the prey's hindquarters next, and then the muscles on the insides of the legs. The mountain lion's back teeth work like scissors to cut through the tough hide and muscles of the prey. Instead of chewing, a mountain lion cuts its food into chunks with its teeth and swallows them whole.

If a mountain lion has not eaten in a long time, it can eat as much as ten pounds of meat at a time.

Five

Most mountain lions live in western states such as California. Those that live in Florida, like this one, are called panthers.

Too Close for Comfort

Whiting Ranch Wilderness Park in Southern California is a great place to ride mountain bikes. The trails wind through scrub oak and cactus, along ridges, and up and down steep ravines. It also happens to be a great mountain lion habitat.

One January afternoon in 2004, Ann Hjelle, a former Marine and a personal trainer, and her friend Debi Nicholls, a mountain bike racer, decided to go for a ride in the park. "Anne was thirty yards ahead of me on the Cactus Trail, which is only a couple of feet wide," Nicholls said later. "I couldn't see her. Suddenly I heard screaming. As I came around the corner I saw this mountain lion. He was on top of her; she was on her back."

Nicholls jumped off her bike and threw it at the mountain lion. The lion was not disturbed. Its jaws gripped Hjelle's head. Hjelle later reported that she did not feel any pain at the time. She was amazed at the power of the animal, which she said seemed to have the strength of ten people. The mountain lion started clamping down, tearing her

Mistaken for Prey

A mountain lion has the instinct and the ability to leap on the back of a prey animal running on four legs. Therefore, a person standing upright and facing a mountain lion presents an awkward target for the predator. On the other hand, mountain lion experts think that people riding bicycles, running, or bending over look more like a mountain lion's normal prey, and may trigger the instinct to attack.

left ear from her skull, ripping one side of her face off, and breaking her nose. Hjelle was sure she was going to die.

Nicholls started kicking the mountain lion and screaming at it to let go of her friend. The mountain lion dragged Hjelle by her neck down the trail and off the path. Nicholls caught up and grabbed Hjelle's left leg and hung on. The mountain lion dragged the two women down the slope thirty or forty feet through the brush, according to Nicholls. "I'd grabbed [Anne's] left leg and I had my right leg digging in the ground and my left leg trying to fend [the mountain lion] off. I never let go because [Anne] would have been out of sight in no time."

Hjelle's face was covered with blood. The mountain lion kept trying to get a better grip with its jaws, going from her helmet, to her face, to her neck. When Hjelle said to her friend that she was going to die, Nicholls answered, "You're not. I will never let go of your leg."

Four men further along the trail heard the women's screams. When they came upon the scene, they saw the tug-of-war between the mountain lion, trying to pull Hjelle away, and Nicholls, holding onto Hjelle's legs, pulling in the other direction. The men started throwing large rocks at the mountain lion. Finally, one of the rocks hit it behind the neck. The animal let go of Hjelle and disappeared into the brush.

The men carried Hjelle back to the trail. Another rider called 911, and soon a helicopter came to take the women to the hospital. Hjelle underwent six hours of surgery while doctors used

Two of the men who came upon Anne Hjelle being attacked by a mountain lion tell their story to a reporter.

two thousand stitches to begin to put her face back together. She had damage to the nerves and muscles in her face, and would require several more surgeries over the next year.

While Hjelle and Nicholls were being airlifted to the hospital, park rangers and police hunted for

The mountain lion was hovering near the body of another bicyclist who had been killed earlier in the day.

Hjelle's attacker. They tracked the mountain lion, and found it near the body of Mark Reynolds, another bicyclist who had been killed earlier in the day near the place where Hjelle was attacked.

Experts were not able to explain why this mountain lion attacked two people in the same day. Some say that it may have been protecting its food. The mountain lion was shot and killed. It was a two-year-old male that weighed 110 pounds. It may have been a mountain lion that had not yet found its own home range.

Rare Encounters

When humans move into mountain lion habitats, deadly encounters can occur. The Whiting Ranch Wilderness Park borders a national forest and several residential areas. Nevertheless, attacks such as the ones on Anne Hjelle and Mark Reynolds are very rare. According to California Fish and Game Department biologist Doug Updike, before the Hjelle and Reynolds attacks there had been only fourteen mountain lion attacks on humans since the 1880s. Six of them were fatal.

Even if the number of encounters is increasing, they are still very rare. Since 1990, the average number of fatal attacks in California is about one every two years.

Researchers put a special collar on a tranquilized mountain lion. The collar allows them to track its movements to learn more about mountain lion behavior.

Six

If you hike in mountain lion territory, make sure you have a plan of what to do in case of an encounter

When a Mountain Lion Attacks

Mountain lions are predators constantly searching for food. They must hunt to survive. For the most part, mountain lions keep their distance from humans. But they have been known to attack humans in the suburbs, in parks near cities, and in the mountains and national forest lands of the West. Attacks are more likely on remote, seldom-used trails or forest roads than in more populated areas. Mountain lions are most active between dusk and dawn, but they have been known to attack during the day as well.

Protecting Yourself

Even though a mountain lion's actions are often unpredictable, there are certain steps you can take to protect yourself. The more you know, the more likely you are to avoid an encounter or to survive an attack.

The best way to avoid an encounter with a mountain lion is to learn about mountain lion behavior. If you live in or near a mountain lion

A mountain lion's daytime vision is not very clear. For this reason, a biker can seem to take the shape of a mountain lion's main prey—a deer.

habitat, do not spend a lot of time outside at dusk, during the night, or at dawn. If you see an animal carcass, especially one that has been covered with leaves and twigs, stay away from it in case it is a mountain lion's kill. The mountain lion will often protect it or come back to feed again.

To avoid an encounter when hiking in mountain lion habitat, travel in groups of two or more, with an adult at the front and the back of a larger group. Make enough noise to warn animals of your presence. Most will avoid people. Keep all dogs on a leash. Dogs do not scare mountain lions away. In fact, they might attract them as easy prey.

It is also useful to hike with a sturdy walking stick, which can be used as a weapon against a mountain lion. Running or jogging is not a good idea because it might trigger a mountain lion's natural instinct to pursue prey. Finally, have a plan for what to do if you see a mountain lion, and make sure everyone in the group knows the plan.

The main thing to keep in mind when facing a mountain lion is to stay alert and do everything you can to convince it you are not an easy meal.

Another thing to keep in mind is that mountain lion attacks are still rare, and should not scare people away from enjoying the outdoors. Understanding the habits of mountain lions will help to keep us safer, and also help us to protect these beautiful and solitary animals as part of our diverse wildlife.

Because a deer and someone riding a bicycle can seem similar in shape to a mountain lion, riders should use extreme caution when biking in mountain lion territory.

If You See a Mountain Lion

The following guidelines, offered by most state and federal wildlife agencies, will help you form your plan. If you see a mountain lion and it has seen you, remember the following:

Do not panic. Remember what you need to do and stay in control of the situation. The mountain lion is a hungry animal doing what comes naturally. It is using all of its knowledge and skills to survive. You should do the same.

Stand up straight. Do not turn your back, crouch, or try to hide. Face the mountain lion so that it knows you have seen it. This makes you seem less like prey.

Make yourself look bigger. Hold your jacket or backpack over your head. If nothing else, raise your arms. The idea is to look like a taller, odd-shaped creature that is confusing to the mountain lion. Remember, a mountain lion's eyes do not focus as well in the daytime as they do at night.

Do not run or turn your back. Keep facing the animal as you move slowly toward safety. If you are with others, back away in a tight group. If there is a car or a building nearby, try to get to it. If not, try to get to higher ground.

If the mountain lion is creeping toward you, follow the above guidelines and also:

Yell, scream, and shout. Let the animal know that you are not prey. Make it think you are dangerous.

Show your teeth. This may make you look more like an attacker than prey.

Finally, if the mountain lion attacks:

Fight back as hard as you can. Try to strike the animal in the eyes, nose, and ears. Use whatever you have, such as a knife, camera, rock, stick, or your fists.

If someone else has been attacked and the mountain lion retreats, do not leave the attacked person alone for a moment, because the animal often returns again and again to try to secure its prey.

Glossary

cache—The food a mountain lion has stored and hidden to come back to later.

camouflage—The color or shape of an animal that helps disguise it in nature.

canine teeth—The long, sharp teeth on either side of the upper and lower front teeth.

carcass—The body of a dead animal.

carnivore—An animal whose diet is made up entirely of meat.

den—A sheltered place where a wild animal makes its home.

habitat—The area in which an animal lives. A suitable habitat includes enough water, food, space, and shelter.

home range—The area in which an individual animal lives, and which it will guard against other animals.

instinct—A way of behaving that is natural to an animal from birth.

predator—An animal that survives by killing and eating other animals.

prey—An animal that is hunted and eaten by another animal.

species—A group of animals with similar characteristics that are able to breed with one another.

undergrowth—Bushes and other low plants that cover the ground.

Books

Becker, John C. *The Florida Panther*. San Diego: KidHaven Press, 2003.

Corrigan, Patricia. *Big Cats*. Chanhassen, Minn.: Northwood Press, 2002.

Gouck, Maura. *Mountain Lions*. Chanhassen, Minn.: The Child's World, 2001.

Smith, David. *Don't Get Eaten*. Seattle: Mountaineers Books, 2003.

Internet Addresses

Big Cats On Line: Puma
<http://dialspace.dial.pipex.com/agarman/bco/ver4.htm>

List of Confirmed Cougar Attacks in the United States and Canada 1890–1990
<http://www.frii.com/~mytymyk/lions/attacks.htm>

Mountain Lion Foundation
<http://www.mountainlion.org>

Index